Wedding inspirations

Wedding inspirations

Creative ideas to celebrate a marriage

Beverley Jollands

HERMES HOUSE

Published in 1999 by Hermes House

HERMES HOUSE books are available for bulk purchase for sales
promotion and for premium use. For details, write or call the sales
director, Hermes House, 27 West 20th Street, New York, NY 10011;
(800) 354-9657

Hermes House is an imprint of
Anness Publishing Inc.

ISBN 1-84038-275-9

Publisher: **Joanna Lorenz**
Project Editor: **Sarah Duffin**
Contributors : **Fiona Barnett, Stephanie Donaldson,
Tessa Evelegh, Lucinda Ganderton, Gilly Love and
Dorothy Wood**
Designer: **Lisa Tai**
Photographers: **Karl Adamson, James Duncan,
Michelle Garrett, Debbie Patterson** and **Polly Wreford**
Illustrator: **Lucinda Ganderton**
Reader: **Penelope Goodare**
Production Controller: **Ben Worley**

Printed and bound in China

10 9 8 7 6 5 4 3 2 1

Contents

The Ceremony

With This Ring I Thee Wed

Bring her up to th'high altar, that she may

The sacred ceremonies there partake,

The which do endless matrimony make.

Edmund Spenser (1552-99), *Epithalamion*

The Bride is Prepared

Up then fair phoenix Bride, frustrate the sun,
    Thyself from thine affection
    Takest warmth enough, and from thine eye
All lesser birds will take their jollity.
    Up, up fair Bride, and call,
Thy stars, from out their several boxes, take
Thy rubies, pearls, and diamonds forth, and make
Thyself a constellation of them all,
    And by their blazing, signify,
That a great Princess falls, but doth not die;
Be thou a new star, that to us portends
Ends of much wonder; and be thou those ends.
Since thou dost this day in new glory shine,
May all men date records, from this thy Valentine.

John Donne (1572-1631), from *An Epithalamion on the Lady Elizabeth and Count Palatine being married on St Valentine's Day*

The Marriage of Queen Victoria and Prince Albert

Had my hair dressed and the wreath of orange flowers put on... I wore a white satin gown with a very deep flounce of Honiton lace, imitation of old. I wore my Turkish diamond necklace and earrings, and Albert's beautiful sapphire brooch... The Ceremony was very imposing, and fine and simple, and I think ought to make an everlasting impression on every one who promises at the Altar to keep what he or she promises. Dearest Albert repeated everything very distinctly. I felt so happy when the ring was put on, and by Albert...

...I went and changed my gown, and then came back to his small sitting room where dearest Albert was sitting and playing... He took me on his knee, and kissed me and was so dear and kind... He called me names of tenderness, I have never yet heard used to me before – was bliss beyond belief! Oh! this was the happiest day of my life! – May God help me to do my duty as I ought and be worthy of such blessings.

Queen Victoria's Journal, 10 February 1840

To the Vicar of Shiplake

Vicar of that pleasant spot,
    Where it was my chance to marry,
Happy, happy be your lot
    In the Vicarage by the quarry:
You were he that knit the knot.

Sweetly, smoothly flow your life.
    Never parish feud perplex you,
Tithe unpaid, or party strife.
    All things please you, nothing vex you;
You have given me such a wife.

Have I seen in one so near
    Aught but sweetness aye prevailing?
Or, through more than half a year,
    Half the fraction of a failing?
Therefore bless you, Drummond dear.

Good she is, and pure and just.
    Being conquered by her sweetness
I shall come through her, I trust,
    Into fuller-orbed completeness;
Though but made of erring dust.

You, meanwhile, shall day by day
    Watch your standard roses blowing,
And your three young things at play
    And your triple terrace growing
Green and greener every May.

Smoothly flow your life with Kate's,
    Glancing off from all things evil,
Smooth as Thames below your gates,
    Thames along the silent level
Streaming through his osiered aits.

Alfred, Lord Tennyson (1809-92)

Good she is, and pure and just.
Being conquered by her sweetness...

My true love hath my heart

My true love hath my heart, and I have his,
By just exchange, one for the other given.
I hold his dear, and mine he cannot miss,
There never was a better bargain driven.
His heart in me keeps me and him in one,
My heart in him his thoughts and senses guides;
He loves my heart, for once it was his own,
I cherish his, because in me it bides.
His heart his wound receivèd from my sight,
My heart was wounded with his wounded heart;
For as from me on him his hurt did light,
So still methought in me his hurt did smart.
Both equal hurt, in this change sought our bliss:
My true love hath my heart and I have his.

Sir Philip Sidney (1554-86)

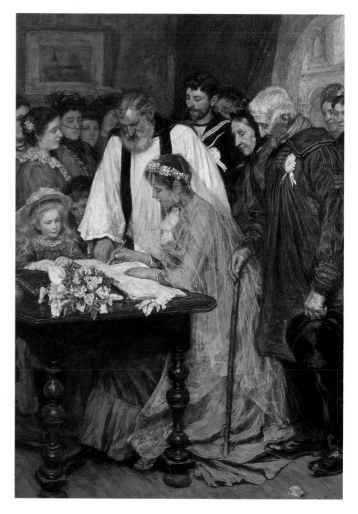

Facing the Future

Methinks this birthday of our married
life is like a cape, which we now have
doubled, and find a more infinite
ocean of love stretching out before us.
God bless us and keep us; for there is
something more awful in happiness
than in sorrow – the latter being
earthly and finite, the former
composed of the texture and
substance of eternity, so that spirits
still embodied may well tremble at it.

Nathaniel Hawthorne (1804-64),
from *The American Notebooks*

Preparing for the Wedding

A marriage is an occasion for great festivity among family and friends, and its celebration has become the focus for more customs and folklore than any other event. All over the world, and in all cultures, time-honoured traditions are observed, as guests gather together to toast the bride and groom.

The convention of a white wedding is comparatively recent: until the 19th century many women simply married in their best dress, which might be any colour. White was associated with virginity, but not specifically with brides. During the American Revolution, republican brides sometimes wore red as a symbol of defiance. Icelandic brides wore black velvet richly embroidered with gold and silver.

Blue was a popular choice as it was associated with purity and fidelity, and the old tradition of wearing blue continues as part of the custom of wearing "something old, something new, something borrowed and something blue" which is still widely followed by brides today. Each of the required elements may be on her

Left: *Romantic floral scents - especially costly essence of rose - calm the nerves as well as enhancing wedding-day euphoria.*

dress or form part of the bride's accessories. The "old" symbolizes the past, the "new" looks to the future and the "borrowed" is a link with the present.

The making of the wedding dress is surrounded by numerous superstitions. The groom must not see the

Above: Ancient tradition dictates that a bride should not look in a mirror before leaving for her wedding to prevent her soul, which is represented by her reflection, from being stolen.

dress until the actual service, and the final stitches should not be put in until just before the bride departs for the

ceremony. Only after the last stitch has been sewn can she put on her veil. Anybody who works on a wedding gown should hide a hair or a small coin inside the hem, and it is said that whoever sews the first stitch will herself be married within the year.

Bouquets and Baskets

In the past, most brides carried wired cascades of flowers, but a more informal arrangement is now more common, sometimes decorated with ribbons. Brides are encouraged by their guests to fling their bouquets into the assembled party, and usually aim them at their bridesmaids: by tradition, whoever catches the flowers is thought to be the next to marry. The choice of flowers is significant and will often include traditional favourites such as white or red roses, gypsophila (baby's breath), lily-of-the-valley and, of course, orange blossom.

The red rose, which the Romans dedicated to Venus, is acknowledged to be the flower of love, the "Queen of Flowers". Its significance changes as it develops: a rosebud signifies the tender beginnings of love, while the

Above: *The intoxicating scent of tuberose and freesia is a great bonus to this delightful basket of creamy-yellow flowers.*

Left: *For young bridesmaids, a basket of flowers is easier to carry than a posy, and little girls will like the cheerful colours of these arrangements, which include sunshine yellow roses and lime-green fennel. If the flowers are arranged in florist's foam they will stay fresh for several days.*

full-blown flower represents the fulfilment of passion.

Orange blossom, with its heady, sensual perfume, represents fertility. It became a fashionable accessory for British and American brides in the 1820s, and was used to garland the wedding dress as well as the bride's hair (the flowers were often made of wax, but real blossoms were used too). When Queen Victoria married Prince Albert in 1840, the wreath she wore was entirely of orange blossom. She carried myrtle in her bouquet, which according to a German tradition would bring harmony to the household. Wedding favours in the form of sprigs of orange blossom, tied with silver lace and satin ribbon, were handed to the distinguished guests as they arrived.

Below: *Ribbon chosen to complement the flowers covers the binding of this brightly coloured bouquet. A hand-tied arrangement can be kept in water until the ceremony, so you can assemble it the day before to allow some of the roses to open a little and fill out the display.*

A Classic Wedding Bouquet

The linear hand-tied bouquet is a very romantic arrangement, perfect for brides with long flowing dresses.
It may be held either pointing downwards or in the curve of an elbow. Yellow and white flowers are synonymous
with spring, and several branches of mimosa add a sharp, sweet fragrance to the bouquet.

- 5 stems 'Yellow Dot' spray roses
- 5 stems 'Tina' spray roses
- 5 stems mimosa
- variegated pittosporum

- 5 stems pale yellow tulips
- 5 stems white tulips
- 5 stems white anemones
- variegated trailing ivy

- scissors
- twine or raffia
- white or pale yellow ribbon

1 Strip all the stems of any leaves and thorns which would be below the binding point (about one-third of the way up each stem). Thorns should be neatly cut off so as not to damage the rose stems. Place a rose, a stem of mimosa and one of pittosporum in one hand to form the centre.

2 Lay each subsequent stem at an angle of 45°. Holding the bouquet in the hand, turn it, always keeping in the same direction to develop the spiral shape and adding further stems as you turn. Hold the stems quite firmly at the binding point while adding new flowers.

3 Twist the twine or raffia just above the hand and tie firmly at the binding point. Trim all the stems to an even length and finish the bouquet with a bow.

Right: The bouquet needs to stand in water for as long as possible before the ceremony. Dry the stems before it is carried by the bride.

Headdresses and Haircombs

Long before the wedding dress became the focus of attention, the headgear worn by brides had acquired plenty of symbolism. A Roman bride wore an all-enveloping yellow veil throughout her wedding, until she reached her new home and could be unveiled by the groom. Underneath, her hair was held in an elaborate arrangement by a special spear-shaped comb, and decorated with a garland of flowers. Anglo-Saxon weddings were performed under a veil held by an attendant, similar to the huppa used today at Jewish weddings.

The veil had been discarded altogether by the 18th century, though garlands of flowers (or jewels) were always worn. It made a comeback with the classical fashions of the Regency period, when it was worn for special occasions by all women, not just brides. It wasn't worn over

Above: Decorative without being cumbersome, this hair comb with fresh flowers makes a delicate adornment for the bride's hair.

Left: Dried roses, grasses, phalaris and tiny starfish make an intriguing hair decoration in subtle, pale colours that would go beautifully with frail old lace.

the face again until the 1860s, when the image of the shy and blushing bride was cultivated. The now traditional practice of arriving for the ceremony veiled and leaving with the veil thrown back came even later.

An old veil is supposed to be luckier than a new one, and it is luckiest of all if it is borrowed from a happily married friend or relation. In some families, a valuable length of lace veils a succession of brides.

Below: *This garland headdress mixes fragrant tuberoses and freesia with fluffy mimosa and golden crab apples. It will sit comfortably on the bride's head without complicated fixings.*

Above: *A rich colour combination, not usually associated with traditional wedding flowers, makes a striking circlet for a bridesmaid: this one uses deep red and apricot roses with flowering mint. Small bunches of rosehips add weight to the design.*

Church Porch Decoration

If you are decorating a church for a wedding, you can create an entrance with impact by arranging a display of flowers and foliage around the porch. You need to plan this kind of decoration on a generous scale if it is to work well, though you can use simple plant materials very successfully.

- 20 bunches long ivy trails
- twine
- scissors
- 6 large bunches rosehips
- natural raffia

1 Drape ivy trails generously over the supporting beam of the porch roof, starting from the outside and working towards the centre. Secure the ivy at regular intervals with twine.

2 When the beam is evenly covered, position the branches of rosehips. Start from the outside again and drape them over the ivy to hang at the front of the porch.

3 Secure the branches of rosehips firmly in position with twine. Form a large bow with the raffia and attach it to the central vertical strut above the rosehips and ivy.

Right: This porch decoration is designed to look natural, almost as though it is growing out of the structure. Flowers would have been lost in the green mass of ivy, so colour contrast has been provided by brilliant red rosehips.

Confetti Box

A hand-made box for confetti is so much prettier to carry than a commercially printed one and can be kept afterwards as a small memento of the day. This lovely box is decorated with enchanting pink-and-gold roses and closed with a ribbon bow.

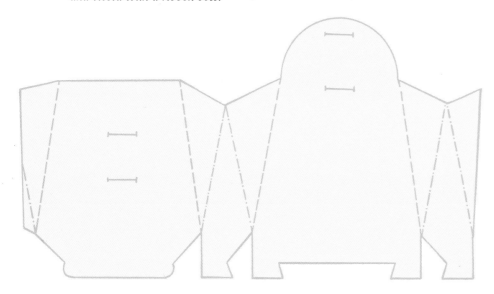

- paper
- pencil
- thin card (cardboard)
- scissors
- paintbrush
- pink acrylic paint
- gold ink
- ruler
- kitchen knife
- cutting mat
- craft knife
- double-sided tape
- ribbon
- rose-petal confetti

1 Copy and enlarge the template above, and transfer the pattern to a sheet of thin card (cardboard). Cut it out. Brush the surface with water, then paint rough, round pink shapes so that the colour bleeds out. When the paint is dry, use gold ink to paint stylized petals and leaf shapes. Allow to dry.

2 Score along the fold lines using a ruler and a blunt knife.

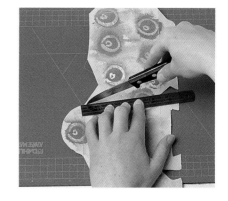

Above: *Pretty and elegant, a rose-decorated box makes the perfect container for paper rose-petals.*

3 Use a craft knife to cut the slits for the ribbon.

4 Cut a piece of double-sided tape and stick it to one side of the tab. Peel off the backing, overlap the tab and stick in place. Fold under the bottom edge and thread the ribbon through the slits. Fill with rose confetti, and then tie the ribbon in a bow.

The
Celebration

High Wedlock Then be Honoured

We will begin these rites,

As we do trust they'll end, in true delights

William Shakespeare (1564-1616), *As You Like It*

A Country Wedding

Fancy caused her looks to wear as much matronly expression as was obtainable out of six hours' experience as a wife, in order that the contrast between her own state of life and that of the unmarried young women present might be duly impressed upon the company: occasionally stealing glances of admiration at her left hand, but this quite privately...

Five country dances, including "Haste to the Wedding", two reels, and three fragments of hornpipes, brought them to the time for supper... At the conclusion of the meal Dick went out to put the horse in; and Fancy, with the elder half of the four bridesmaids, retired upstairs to dress for the journey to Dick's new cottage near Mellstock.

...Amid a medley of laughter, old shoes, and elder-wine, Dick and his bride took their departure side by side in the excellent new spring-cart which the young tranter now possessed.

Thomas Hardy (1840-1928), *Under the Greenwood Tree*

The Ensilver Song

Now here's a good health to the bride of yon house,
Grant her a solid good cheer;
Lord, bless her good health, Lord, prosper her wealth,
That we may be married next year.

Well, here's to the bride, good luck to the lass,
Grant her a solid good cheer;
And through her garter we'll pass each glass,
And may we be married next year.

Our glasses we'll lift now to the bridegroom,
Grant him a solid good cheer;
And the fellow that spills it he'll pay for t'next round,
And may we be married next year.

To the bridal pair we all will sing,
And grant them a solid good cheer;
In spite of Turk or Spanish king,
And may we be married next year.

Traditional Yorkshire song

On an Island

You've pluck'd a curlew, drawn a hen,
Wash'd the shirts of seven men,
You've stuffed my pillow, stretch'd the sheet,
And fill'd the pan to wash your feet,
You've coop'd the pullets, wound the clock,
And rinsed the young men's drinking crock;
And now we'll dance to jigs and reels,
Nailed boots chasing girls' naked heels,
Until your father'll start to snore,
And Jude, now you're married, will stretch on the floor.

J. M. Synge (1871-1909)

On Marriage

Love one another, but make not a bond of love:

Let it rather be a moving sea between the shores of your souls.

Fill each other's cup, but drink not from one cup.

Give one another of your bread, but eat not from the same loaf.

Sing and dance together and be joyous, but let each one of you be alone,

Even as the strings of a lute are alone though they quiver with the same music.

Give your hearts, but not into each other's keeping:

For only the hand of Life can contain your hearts.

And stand together yet not too near together:

For the pillars of the temple stand apart,

And the oak tree and the cypress grow not in each other's shadow.

Kahlil Gibran, *The Prophet* (1883-1931)

Cutting the Wedding Cake

Just as traditional as the ceremony itself, the reception provides an opportunity for the bride's and groom's relatives and friends to meet and share in the couple's happiness.

After the formal toasts, the main event is the cutting of the wedding cake. The bride and groom usually cut the first slice from the wedding cake together, making a wish as they do so. Absolutely everyone must have a piece. The top layer is often saved and stored away for the christening of the first child.

Bride-cakes were once dry biscuits made to be broken over the bride's head. Elizabethan cooks improved the recipe, adding eggs, sugar and

Right: It is the usual practice to set the cake on a small table of its own, where it is clearly visible for the traditional cutting of the cake.

fruit, but the result was still thrown at the bride, or crumbled over her. The familiar tiered confections of icing, columns, cherubs, bells, horseshoes and flowers follow a style set by the Victorians. In 19th-century America it became the vogue to have two cakes: one for the bride and one for the groom. A lucky wedding ring was sometimes baked into the cake. Whoever found it was guaranteed happiness for the next twelve months.

Above: Dress the wedding table in white, like the bride, with layers of muslin and a froth of tulle. Using plain white and cream china, different shapes can be mixed and matched if you have to borrow extra pieces to cater for a large number. Fruit and flowers in fresh tones of green and white make harmonious decorations.

Heart-frosted Glasses

Frosting makes a quick and easy decoration for glasses, but is normally restricted to the rim. On a romantic occasion such as a wedding, you can take the idea a step further by frosting a heart on the side of each glass. The frosting is remarkably resilient and will last well throughout the party.

- 2 saucers
- fine paintbrush
- lightly beaten egg white
- glasses
- caster (superfine) sugar
- short lengths of narrow white ribbon

1 Dip the paintbrush into the egg white, paint a heart shape on to the glass, and fill in the shape with plenty of egg white.

2 Sprinkle caster sugar on the painted heart: it will stick to the egg white. Shake off the excess sugar.

3 Dip the rim of the glass into the egg white, then into the sugar. Shake off the excess sugar. Tie a length of ribbon around the stem of the glass and finish with a small bow.

A delicate bow tied around the stem of the glass adds a pretty finishing touch.

Carved Pear Centrepiece

The natural beauty of fruit makes it perfect for a restrained table decoration.

• 3 pears
• sharp paring knife
• fresh lemon juice
• tazza or cake stand

Remove vertical strips of skin from each fruit and coat the peeled areas with lemon juice to stop them discolouring. Arrange the pears on the cake stand.

Right: Conference pears become elegant sculptures when selectively peeled to reveal stripes of creamy flesh.

Tulle Party Favour

Enhance the table decoration with one of these little bundles for each guest.

• 15 cm/6 in square tissue paper
• 15 cm/6 in square white tulle
• silver dragées or sugared almonds
• 15 cm/6 in narrow white ribbon

Lay the tissue paper on top of the tulle. Place the sugared almonds in the centre, then gather up and tie with the ribbon.

Right: Tulle-wrapped favours are charming, traditional keepsakes and look pretty when made to match the table decoration.

Celebratory Table Decoration

A table set for a wedding feast doesn't usually have much room to spare on it. Here, the wine cooler has been displayed on a small separate table, surrounded by a sumptuous, textural display of gold, yellow and white flowers with green and grey foliage. The silver is enhanced by the beauty of the decoration, and in turn its highly polished surface reflects the flowers to increase their impact.

- 40 cm / 16 in diameter florist's foam ring
- scissors
- 12 stems *Senecio laxifolius*
- 15 stems elaeagnus

- 3 pairs of chestnuts
- stub (floral) wires
- thick gloves
- wire cutters
- 18 stems yellow roses

- 10 stems cream *Eustoma grandiflorum*
- 10 stems solidago
- 10 stems flowering fennel

1 Soak the foam ring in water. Cut the senecio stems to 14 cm/5½ in and distribute around the ring to create an even foliage outline. Leave the centre of the ring clear.

2 Cut the elaeagnus stems to 14 cm/5½ in and distribute evenly throughout the senecio to reinforce the foliage outline, still leaving the centre of the foam ring clear.

3 Wearing gloves, push stub (floral) wires through the three chestnut pairs, twist the ends together and trim to about 6 cm/2½ in. Position them at three equidistant points around the ring.

Right: A polished silver wine cooler looks magnificent in the centre of a golden floral ring.

4 Cut the rose stems to about 14 cm/5½ in and arrange them in staggered groups of three at six points around the ring, equal distances apart.

5 Cut stems of single eustoma flower heads 12 cm/4¾ in long and arrange evenly in the ring. Cut the stems of solidago to about 14 cm/5½ in and distribute throughout. Finally, cut the stems of fennel to about 12 cm/4¾ in and add evenly through the display.

The Wedding Breakfast

Until 1885, all church weddings had to be conducted before noon, unless they were held by special licence. It was an old custom to be married early in the day, so that the feast that followed could actually be described as breakfast. The wedding breakfast was, in effect, the first meal of the couple's new life, but now that most celebrations are held later in the day this term for the reception has fallen into disuse.

Feasting is an integral part of the celebration of marriage. In medieval times, the "bride-ale" was held in the church itself immediately after the religious ceremony: the assembled company was given a party but expected to contribute to its cost, and with luck there would be enough left

Above: If you have to use a wide-necked container that offers little support for flowers, tie the arrangement into a generous posy before standing it in the bowl. The bride's own bouquet could be used in this way as an elegant centrepiece for the reception.

Left: *The symbolism of weddings extends even to these Victorian ceramic cake supports. The female figure represents Ceres, goddess of the harvest and source of fertility, the ivy twining round the pillar stands for the ties of marriage, and the Cupids are bringers of love and romance.*

over from the collection to give the couple's married life a good start. Later, in the 17th century these celebrations moved out of the church into a nearby tavern, and huge numbers were invited.

In country areas, a wedding was as much an excuse for a sporting event

Above: *Thick pillar candles will burn for hours, so are ideal for a wedding party that will go on into the night.*

as a party, with races and dancing. There was a reward for the first guest to reach the bride's home after the ceremony. Since this might be some distance from the church, it could be

a hard-fought race. The prize was a cup of porridge, cabbage soup, or a bride cake. This cake was stuck on a long pole, called the bride-stake, which was erected outside the bride's house. The winner was the person who managed to knock the cake down with a stick.

Spring Napkin Decoration

The sophisticated gold and white colour combination used in these elegant and delicate napkin decorations would be perfect for a wedding. In addition to its exquisite scent, the tiny bells of lily-of-the-valley visually harmonize with the pure white of the cyclamen.

For each napkin:
- sprig of small-leaved ivy
- scissors

- 4-5 stems lily-of-the-valley
- 3 stems dwarf cyclamen (*Cyclamen persicum*)

- 3 cyclamen leaves
- gold cord

1 Fold each napkin into a rectangle, then roll into a cylindrical shape. Wrap an ivy sprig around the middle of the napkin. Tie the stem firmly in a knot.

2 Take the lily-of-the-valley and cyclamen flowers and create a small sheaf in your hand by spiralling the stems. Place one cyclamen leaf at the back of the flowers for support, and two more around the cyclamen flowers to emphasize the focal point. Tie at the binding point with gold cord. Lay the flat back of the sheaf on top of the napkin and ivy, and wrap the excess gold cord around the napkin, gently tying it into a bow on top of the stems.

Right: *Lily-of-the-valley, with its virginal white bells, is a traditional bridal flower for a spring wedding.*

Wedding Favour Basket

This heart-shaped basket is decorated with a selection of white flowers – alstroemeria, ranunculus, roses and phlox – to form a table decoration for the reception. One could be filled with sugared almond favours for the guests at each table.

- scissors
- 10 heads white alstroemeria 'Ice Cream'
- 10 heads white ranunculus
- 10 heads white spray rose 'Princess'

- 10 clusters small, white phlox buds 'Rembrandt'
- 1 bunch pittosporum
- fine stub (floral) wires
- florist's (stem-wrap) tape

- 1 heart-shaped loose-weave basket
- florist's reel wire

1 Cut all the flower and foliage stems to about 2.5 cm/1 in. You will need about 25 small stems of pittosporum. Mount all the elements on fine stub (floral) wires and wrap with florist's (stem-wrap) tape. Lay out your materials, ready to decorate the basket one side at a time.

2 Lay a stem of pittosporum at the centre top of the heart shape. Stitch florist's reel wire through the basket and over the pittosporum stem. Stitch a bud of alstroemeria over the foliage, followed by a rose head, more pittosporum, a ranunculus head and a cluster of phlox.

3 Repeat this sequence until you reach the bottom point, then stitch through the basket weave to secure. Decorate the other side of the basket, working in the opposite direction.

Right: A symbolically romantic heart-shaped basket is the perfect container for party favours.

Gifts
and Love Tokens

That's for Remembrance

This votive pledge of fond esteem,

    Perhaps dear girl! for me thou'lt prize;

It sings of Love's enchanting dream,

    A theme we never can despise.

Lord Byron (1788-1824), *Stanzas to a Lady*

The Groom's Gift

Sophie called me upstairs to look at my
wedding-dress, which they had just
brought; and under it in the box I found
your present – the veil which, in your
princely extravagance, you sent for from
London: resolved, I suppose, since I
would not have jewels, to cheat me into
accepting something as costly. I smiled as
I unfolded it, and devised how I would tease you about your aristocratic tastes,
and your efforts to mask your plebeian bride in the attributes of a peeress.

Charlotte Brontë (1816-55), *Jane Eyre*

A New Year's Gift

Accept, my love, as true a heart
   As ever lover gave:
'Tis free, it vows, from any art,
   And proud to be your slave.

Then take it kindly, as 'twas meant,
   And let the giver live,
Who, with it, would the world have sent,
   Had it been his to give.

And, that Dorinda may not fear
   I e'er will prove untrue,
My vows shall, ending with the year,
   With it begin anew.

Matthew Prior (1664-1721)

To his wife Mary,
11 August 1810

Every day every hour every moment makes me feel more deeply how blessed we are in each other, how purely how faithfully how ardently, and how tenderly we love each other; I put this last word last because, though I am persuaded that a deep affection is not uncommon in married life, yet I am confident that a lively, gushing, thought-employing, spirit-stirring, passion of love is very rare even among good people...

   O Mary I love you with a passion of love which grows till I tremble to think of its strength.

William Wordsworth (1770-1850)

Every day every hour every moment makes me feel more deeply how blessed we are in each other...

Romantic Gifts for the Bride

A wedding is a time when people tend to buy practical household items for the couple, perhaps choosing from a list prepared by the bride herself. Time-honoured gifts are linen, china or glass. But it can also be a wonderful opportunity to continue the tradition of making special romantic items for the bride's trousseau.

The word "trousseau" literally means little bundle, and traditionally it consisted of the clothes and linen that a girl collected together in the months or even years before she married to take to her new home. Over the years other people added extra gifts, from simple good luck

Right: *A modern bride's "trousseau" might include some luxurious underwear lovingly embroidered by a close friend.*

tokens such as decorative horseshoes or spoons, to luxurious garments such as evening gowns and lingerie. A wedding shower, a party given before the wedding at which the bride's close friends give her presents, is an appealing American idea that is becoming increasingly popular elsewhere.

In 19th-century America, the bride's friends would sometimes join together to make her a commemorative quilt. This was known as an "album" quilt, with each person con-

Above: A wedding is a unique celebration of love, and every bride will treasure mementoes of her special day, from her dress and shoes to her flowers and the decorations on her cake.

tributing an individual block. Baltimore in particular became famous for its richly patterned patchwork and appliqué. A British wedding quilt of the same period, in contrast to these exuberantly coloured examples, was covered in a single sheet of plain fabric. The outline of the quilting design was drawn

on the cloth and the group of friends would then join in working the intricate, interlaced pattern.

It is the picturesque and popular custom for the bride's attire to include "something old, something new, something borrowed and something blue", and this can be incorporated into a charming gift for her by combining old lace, new ribbons and beads borrowed from a friend, with her initial or perhaps a small motif embroidered in blue.

Keepsakes for the Wedding Guests

Above: *Rose petals, ears of corn and fragrant strewing herbs were the forerunners of confetti, scattered by the bride's friends across her path as she approached the church. Rice was thrown after the newly married couple on their departure.*

An Italian tradition is to make almond favours, or bonbonnières, for the guests at the wedding reception. Five sugared almonds are bound up in layers of gauzy fabric to symbolize health, wealth, happiness, long life and fertility. The favours can form part of the place setting for each guest, or be designed as a centrepiece and distributed at the end of the meal. Traditional Scottish wedding cakes are liberally adorned with small silver charms such as shoes, bells and horseshoes so that every guest can be given one as a favour.

Passing a small piece of wedding cake nine times through the ring is said to endow it with particular magic: put under the pillow it will make an unmarried girl dream of her future husband. Since it is also

unlucky to remove a wedding ring once on the finger, Victorian brides-maids were given the job of threading pieces of cake the day before the wedding. Little boxes containing slices of cake are sometimes mailed as mementoes to friends and relations unable to attend the wedding.

Above: *The crescent shape of the horseshoe is an ancient symbol of growth and good luck. Along with cherubs, hearts and flowers, it has long been a favourite motif for wedding cake decorations, which are sometimes distributed to the guests as lucky charms. Shoes are another lucky symbol and tiny silver versions often decorate the cake. Old boots or shoes are still tied to the bride and groom's car, or thrown after it, as their guests cheer them on to their new life.*

Right: *Bonbonnières, or almond favours, are easy to assemble from tulle, lace or organza. These are made in the classic wedding colours of white and silver.*

Bridal Heart

Pink satin and lace are the essence of femininity; this delicate favour, made of lace embellished with tiny sequins and pearls, would be a lovely small gift to offer a bride on her wedding day.

- paper for template
- pencil
- scissors
- 40 x 20 cm/16 x 8 in pink satin
- 20 cm/8 in square lace fabric or lace mat
- pins
- tacking (basting) thread
- needle
- matching sewing thread
- ready-made silk flowers (optional)
- 3mm/⅛ in flat sequins
- seed pearls
- sewing machine
- polyester wadding (batting)
- 60cm/24 in narrow lace edging
- several short lengths 3mm/⅛ in satin ribbon in complementary colours

1 Copy the heart template and enlarge to the size required. Cut out two hearts from pink satin, allowing a 1 cm/½ in seam allowance all around. Place one under the lace fabric or mat and move it about to find the most attractive pattern area. Pin, then tack (baste) in place. Cut it out, following the outline of the satin.

2 Cut flowers and other motifs from the remaining lace and sew to the centre of the lace, or use silk flowers. Add sequins and pearls. Pin the hearts together, right sides facing. Stitch around the edge, leaving a 5 cm/2 in gap. Trim seams, clip curves and turn through. Fill with wadding (batting) and slip-stitch the gap.

3 Run a gathering thread along the straight edge of the lace edging and pin one end to the top of the heart. Adjusting the gathers evenly, pin the lace all around the outside edge and slip-stitch firmly in place with invisible stitches. Remove the gathering thread. Finish by adding a hanging loop and small ribbon bows.

Right: Let the design of the lace dictate the additional decoration you choose to complete this extravagantly pretty heart.

Tokens and Keepsakes

The textile arts are traditionally a means of demonstrating care and companionship, and women have always used their skills to make such gifts for their friends and family, stitching personal tokens to show their affection. The outpouring of feeling that everyone experiences when a wedding is planned is a great inspiration for such special gifts. Long-hoarded fragments of antique silk or lace, sequins, beads and artificial flowers can be transformed into exquisite keepsakes. These will always remind a bride of the good wishes that went into their making, as well as being a wonderful souvenir of her wedding day, especially if they are embroidered with the couple's initials and the date.

The age-old emblems of love and romance – hearts and flowers – are perfectly appropriate to the enjoyable sentimentality that these presents will evoke in years to come. The heart is a

Above: *A small piece of antique lace can be carefully mounted on a padded silk cushion. Disguise any worn areas of the fabric by sewing on extra motifs from the remaining lace, and add beads, sequins and a posy of silk flowers and ribbons. A little pot-pourri included in the stuffing will give the cushion a delicious scent.*

Left: *Fill a muslin and lace heart with lavender or rose-petal pot-pourri to make a romantic scented sachet for a lingerie drawer.*

universal symbol, recognized the world over as "the source of love and the centre of the soul", so any heart-shaped gift has a special meaning. Even an object with a useful function, such as a pincushion or a little bag, should be as frilly and pretty as possible, as unashamedly romantic as a Victorian Valentine's Day card.

Below: *For a heart-shaped souvenir with a real feel of the countryside, bind a handful of hay around a wire frame with interlaced ribbons and decorate it with carefully dried garden flowers. This is a lovely way to use the best of summer's harvest of roses.*

Above: *This little beaded silk bag is just big enough to hold a lace handkerchief, a lipstick and one or two other essentials. It could be made as a present for the bride, in fabric to match her wedding dress, or as an accessory for each of the bridesmaids, to be carried with, or instead of, a posy.*

Bride's Garter

The tradition of lucky wedding garters dates back many centuries. Elizabethan brides wore garters festooned with multi-coloured ribbons. This contemporary adaptation in alluring lace and silk is bound to bring good fortune to a bride as it incorporates elements that are old, new, borrowed and blue.

- 10 × 90 cm/4 × 36 in pale blue silk
- sewing machine
- matching sewing thread
- safety pin
- iron
- 50 cm/20 in elastic, 3 cm/1½ in wide

- needle
- 1.5 m/1½ yd lace edging, 5 cm/2 in wide
- crystal rocaille embroidery beads
- translucent blue and pearlized 5 mm/½ in cup sequins

- pins
- 45 cm/18 in light blue satin ribbon, 3 mm/⅛ in wide
- 30 cm/12 in cream satin ribbon, 5 mm/½ in wide
- old button

1 Fold the silk in half lengthways and stitch the long edge taking a 1 cm/¹⁄₂ in seam allowance. Attach a safety pin to one end and feed through the tube to turn through. Press lightly so that the seam lies at the back.

2 Fasten the safety pin to one end of the elastic and draw through the silk tube. Stitch the ends firmly together. Turn in the raw edges of the silk and slip-stitch the two ends together.

3 Cut two 60 cm/24 in lengths of lace edging. Join the ends of each piece to form a circle and decorate with beads and sequins, picking out the details of the pattern.

4 Run a gathering thread along each straight edge of lace and draw up to the size of the garter. Even out fullness, pin and oversew the lace on to the silk. Remove gathering thread.

5 Stitch the ends of the remaining piece of lace together. Gather tightly along the straight edge to form a rosette and secure. Cut streamers of blue and cream satin ribbon and sew on to the back of the rosette.

6 Stitch the rosette to the garter and finish by decorating with the old button for good luck.

Above: The beaded frill of this heavenly garter is made from specially designed wedding lace which is intricately decorated with motifs of bells and bows.

Good Luck Charm

The gift of a wooden spoon is said to be a symbol of future harmony, to be carried by the bride on her wedding day and then kept in her kitchen. If you know the bride happens to hate cooking, you could decorate a lucky horseshoe instead – make sure it is carried with the open end upwards to prevent the good fortune from running out.

- wooden spoon
- fine-grade sandpaper
- water-based paint in white, gold and bronze
- paintbrush
- 40 cm/16 in gold gauze ribbon, 2.5 cm/1 in wide

- matching sewing thread
- needle
- scissors
- 70 cm/28 in cream satin ribbon, 8 mm/⅜ in wide
- 40 cm/16 in pale gold satin ribbon, 8 mm/⅜ in wide

- 70 cm/28 in cream satin ribbon, 2 cm/¾ in wide
- pink and cream fabric flowers
- pearl beads
- good luck charm

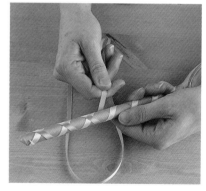

1 Smooth down any rough areas on the spoon using fine-grade sandpaper. Coat the bowl of the spoon with a light layer of white paint, allow to dry, then colourwash with gold. Paint a narrow bronze line around the rim. Leave to dry.

2 Secure the gold gauze ribbon at the top of the handle with a few small stitches and bind it down the handle in a spiral. Finish off just above the bowl of the spoon with another stitch and neatly trim the end.

3 Fasten one end of the 8 mm/⅜ in cream ribbon to the top of the spoon and bind down the handle to cover the edges of the gold gauze. Secure and trim at the lower end, then bind the handle with 8 mm/⅜ in gold ribbon in the opposite direction, so that the spiral neatly crosses the cream ribbon.

4 Cut a 30 cm/12 in length of 8 mm/³⁄₈ in cream ribbon and stitch to the top of the spoon to form a loop. Cover the raw ends at each end of the handle with 10 cm/4 in lengths of wide cream ribbon, stitched in place.

5 Tie the remaining wide cream ribbon into a bow and trim the raw ends into V-shapes. Sew the bow to the spoon just above the bowl. Make streamers from folded lengths of the remaining ribbons and stitch to the cream ribbon band under the bow.

6 Remove the plastic centres from the fabric flowers and replace with pearl beads. Attach flowers around the ribbon band so that the spoon looks attractive from both sides. Stitch a good luck charm to the bow.

Above: *Decorate a wooden spoon with cream silk binding, fabric flowers and pearls to make a traditional lucky charm for the bride.*

Treasured Mementoes and Anniversaries

Long after the useful wedding gifts – the saucepans, toasters and table-cloths – have worn out and been replaced, the bride and groom will usually keep some small mementoes of the day of their marriage. Sweet nothings they gave each other, or keepsakes given by special friends and relatives, will be lovingly tucked away in a cupboard or drawer, to be brought out occasionally with a surge of nostalgia and sentimental pleasure.

The all-important photographs recapture the look, the feeling and the atmosphere of the day, and are every bit as fascinating for children and grandchildren as for the participants themselves. Even more potent are the unconsidered trifles: a silver horse-shoe from the wedding cake, a few fragments of confetti, a dried rose from the bride's bouquet, tickets and receipts collected on the honeymoon. Treasured even at the time they are acquired, these little souvenirs gain tremendous sentimental value over the course of the marriage, and deserve to be carefully preserved.

Left: *A silk-covered Victorian-style album, decorated with beading and braid, is a suitably romantic receptacle for precious wedding photographs, or a safe place to keep wedding and honeymoon memorabilia.*

Above: *A gold-fringed box topped by a trumpeting cherub is the perfect hiding place for the invitations, preserved flowers, cake decorations and other ephemera that are bound to be collected as souvenirs of a special day. The box is lined with taffeta and edged with lace, and makes an imaginative gift for a bride-to-be, who is bound to treasure it.*

List of Anniversaries

Long tradition assigns particular gifts to each anniversary. During the early years, useful items supply the household needs that may not have been fully met by the wedding presents. But as time goes on, the couple's enduring relationship deserves to be saluted by increasingly precious gifts.

first	cotton
second	paper
third	leather
fourth	silk
fifth	wood
sixth	iron
seventh	wool
eighth	bronze
ninth	pottery
tenth	tin
fifteenth	crystal
twentieth	china
twenty-fifth	silver
thirtieth	pearl
thirty-fifth	coral
fortieth	ruby
forty-fifth	sapphire
fiftieth	gold
fifty-fifth	emerald
sixtieth	diamond

Index and Acknowledgements

ACKNOWLEDGEMENTS
The following pictures are reproduced
with kind permission of E.T. Archive:
pp 6-7 and p 12, p 30.
From The Bridgeman Art Library,
London: p 9, p 31, p 44, pp 44-45,
p 46 and p 47.
From Fine Art Photographic Library
Limited: p 6, p 8, p 11, p 13, pp 26-7, p 28,
p 29 and pp 48-9.
From Tony Stone Images: p 32 (R. Weller)